D0913074

This book belongs to

_____

This book is dedicated to my children - Mikey, Kobe, and Jojo. Remember to always be kind.

Masked Ninja

By Mary Nhin

Pictures by
Jelena Stupar

Masks are surgical masks that doctors wear. It helps protect them by creating a barrier to viruses and bacteria.

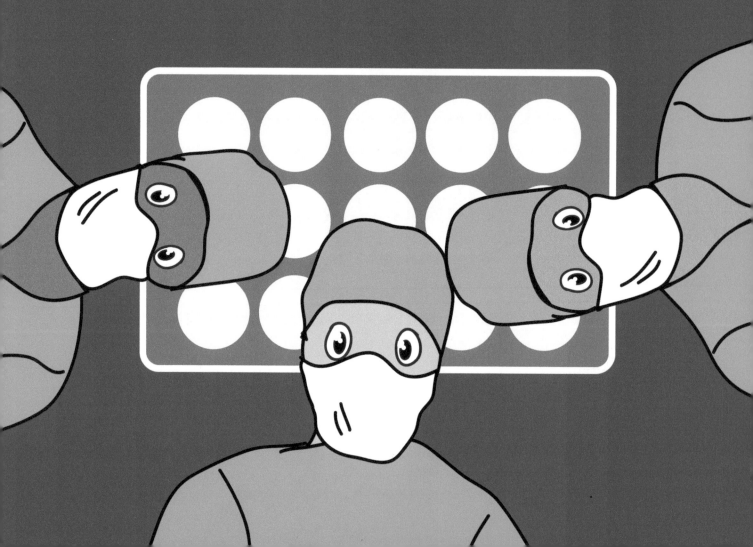

Viruses can make you feel unwell.

Sometimes, it can cause you to become very sick.

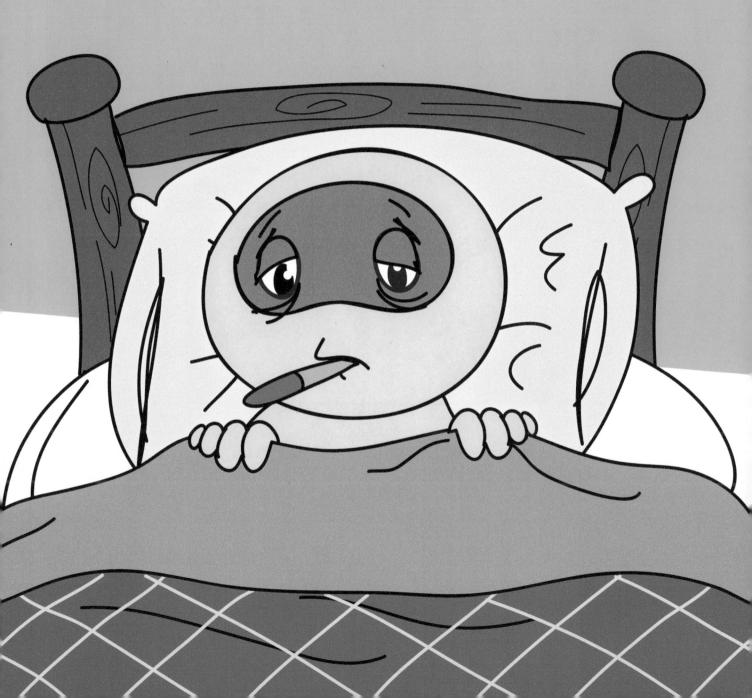

The latest virus is causing everyone around the globe to fall sick. When this happens, it's called a pandemic.

According to the CDC (Center for Disease Control), this virus began in Wuhan City, China.

Viruses are spread when someone coughs, sneezes, or comes in close contact with a person infected with the virus.

Sickness comes in like a landslide, but goes out as slow as spinning silk.

病来如山倒, 病去如抽丝

This is a popular Chinese saying and it is similar to what is happening when there's a pandemic.

All of a sudden, the new virus is spreading quickly, but treating, preventing, and containing it will be very slow and difficult.

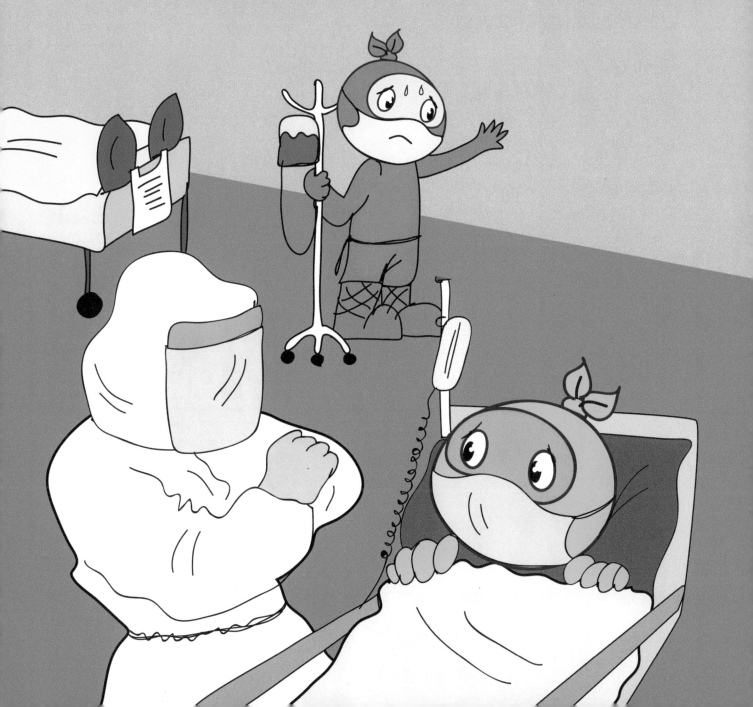

Besides wearing a mask and keeping a safe distance from people, one way to prevent the spread of viruses is to wash your hands.

To do this correctly, it's good to wash often with soap and water for at least 20 seconds.

Another thing you can do is to keep your hands away from your face.

On average, we touch our face more than 100 times a day.

Sneezing into your elbow or a tissue shows respect for other people by protecting them from your germs.

And remember to cover your mouth when you cough.

It's best to cough into a tissue, but if you don't have one using your upper sleeve is good.

There are a lot of rumors on the internet about viruses that cause pandemics. You should only listen to your doctor, CDC, or the WHO.

WHO stands for the World Health Organization.

They are reliable sources of information about viruses.

Some ninjas are teased for causing the virus.

If you're experiencing harassment, you should report it to an adult.

We are all in this together so it's important to be kind to each other.

Remembering these tips could be your secret weapon against the spread of viruses and racism.

Fun, free printables at NinjaLifeHacks.tv

 @marynhin @GrowGrit
#NinjaLifeHacks

 Mary Nhin Grow Grit

 Grow Grit